Lettuce Amaze You
100% Dairy, Gluten, Soy, Nightshade and Grain Free Lettuce Recipes
By Paula C. Henderson

D1784503

Copyright Page

Lettuce Amaze You
100% Dairy, Gluten, Soy, Nightshade and Grain Free Lettuce Recipes

Contents

Introduction

Lettuce? That's right. Lettuce. Leafy greens. Not just salads either. Green leafy vegetables aren't just gaining in popularity with the re-discovered backyard gardens or the popularity of container gardening on the patio. We are finding out just how nutritious and vital they really are to our overall health.

Are you thinking just salads? You're wrong! Salads are great, don't get me wrong, but what about a sauté? How about creamy soup? Have you tried a lettuce cup or a lettuce bun? Did you know you can make sauces and dips out of your lettuce? Hot and Cold?

Lettuce, and all Leafy Greens are naturally low in sodium and a low carb food while offering great health benefits. Lettuce is:

- dairy free
- grain free
- gluten free
- soy free
- nightshade free

As are every single one of the recipes included here in this book. This book is a companion to the 5 Points Diet Plan #5ptsfreediet

With this in mind, Nutritionist and Author Paula C. Henderson, creator of the 5 Points Diet, wrote this book. An encouragement, if you will, to eat at least one leafy green serving every day.

In this book you will find:

- Types of Lettuce and a description of what they taste like.
- Health Benefits of Lettuce and Other Leafy Greens
- Lettuce Cups and The Lettuce Bun Ideas
- Lettuce and Greens You Can Cook
- Salads
- Lettuce Recipes
- Other Leafy Greens You Should Eat

Enjoy these recipes, preparation ideas and the long term health benefits that will come from incorporating more lettuce into your regular diet.

Make this your year. Your milestone year. The beginning of a healthier YOU year. To do your best you have to first feel your best. Start where you are. Start right now.

Because eating vegetables shouldn't be weird.

Types of Lettuce

1. **Arugula:**

   A tender lettuce with a peppery taste. Nice lettuce for a mixed green salad. Goes well with a vinaigrette.

2. **Bibb:**

   A mild tasting lettuce with a tender texture similar to spinach.

3. **Endive:**

   Mildly bitter taste. The lighter the leaves, the more mild the taste. Texture is tender but firm so a great choice for dipping.

4. **Frisee:**

   Slightly peppery taste. Tender leaves. Best served cold. Great for a mixed greens salad and for use in making a pesto.

5. **Iceberg:**

   A bright crisp mild lettuce. Refreshing and watery. Great choice for use in homemade salad dressings, dips and sauces. Great choice when making lettuce cups. Contrary to what we are told this lettuce is nutritious and very hydrating. Great for dry skin, induces a sense of well being when eaten on a regular basis.

6. **Kale:**

   A dark green hearty, leafy green. Taste is a bit milder than spinach. Perfectly okay to purchase fresh or frozen (without sauces or spice). Great to keep on hand as a freezer staple and then buy fresh as a recipe may call for it. Okay to eat raw or cooked but please note: if you have thyroid disease you should limit consumption to cooked kale and avoid raw. The reason? It is a cruciferous vegetable. Cruciferous vegetables are fine for consumption if you have thyroid disease; just cook first.

7. **Leaf Lettuce:**

   Very similar to iceberg only leafy-er (is that a word?) More tender than iceberg perhaps but still firm enough to use as a "bun" for a chicken sandwich or a hamburger. A very mild taste; though not as sweet as iceberg. Cost is about the same as iceberg so try this the next time you are at the store. There are two varieties: red and green. Both are a beautiful leafy green! The green has a slight increase in nutrients over the red variety. This leafy green variety looks beautiful on a sandwich.

8. Radicchio:

   Another variety that is great for sitting out with dip. A beautiful food. Taste is bitter/peppery. Great choice if you are creating a mixed greens salad. Firm crisp leaves. Great in slaws. You can enjoy this cooked or raw.

9. Romaine:

   A popular lettuce. Crisp, bright, mildly sweet taste. Great for lettuce cups and to serve with a dip. Great to use as a base when making homemade salad dressings, Caesar Salads are made with Romaine lettuce. Romaine hearts are also pretty good on the grill.

10. Spinach:

    A tender, dark leaf. We are all familiar with how versatile this vegetable is. I prefer fresh spinach from the produce department and chopped kale when buying frozen. Just a preference.

11. Watercress:

    Watercress has a strong peppery taste, similar to mustard greens. The leaves are tender, not crisp. Generally good with a sweet and sour profile and vinaigrettes which compliments the bitter leaves of the watercress.

Health Benefits of Eating Lettuce and Leafy Greens

Most lettuce varieties are made up of over 70% water. Yes, including iceberg!

This is good news. This means when you eat lettuce you are eating your water. Very hydrating on a warm day or when you are tired, fatigued and need to feel refreshed. This translates into a very healthy snack choice. Just eat like you would celery. A great pick-me-up in the afternoon or after a workout. Every part of your body needs water to function properly. Eating lettuce everyday will help your body stay hydrated.

Approximately 60% of your body weight is water and that ratio needs to be maintained for optimal health. We lose water by:

- Sweating
- Urinating
- blood loss
- diarrhea
- vomiting
- infections in the body
- by not consuming enough water on a daily basis

... And the amount of water can become imbalanced by the amount of sodium we consume as well as medications and supplements we take. How much water each person needs will differ because of our unique lifestyles, activity levels, medications, other food consumptions and body DNA.

You can eat your water just like you can drink your water. This is great news for those of you who tend to not drink water.

If you have a job that does not allow you to drink water throughout the day or you are simply one of those people who does not want to chug water all day or be up all night urinating there is a way to strike a balance. Eating your water by way of foods, such as lettuce, is kind of like a slow release method and your body appreciates and uses this water just like a normal glass of water.

People find the more foods like lettuce they eat that contain higher amounts of water, the less they feel thirsty and the less often they find themselves dehydrated. Being even slightly dehydrated can cause minor headaches, blurred vision, moodiness, fatigue, a feeling of restlessness, dry skin, itchy eyes and more.

Eating a minimum of one serving of lettuce per day can have a healthy compounding effect on the body. Green leafy vegetables, like lettuce, acts as an anti-inflammatory to the body, protecting brain cells, lowering cholesterol levels, induces relaxation which can result in better sleep and controlling anxiety, improves metabolism and helps to balance moods.

That is so important to know lets repeat it one more time:

Eating a minimum of one serving of lettuce per day can have a healthy, compounding effect on the body. Green leafy vegetables, like lettuce, acts as an anti-inflammatory to the body, protecting brain cells, lowering cholesterol levels, inducing relaxation, which can result in a better night's sleep and controlling ones anxiety, improving metabolism and helping to balance moods.

There are many different varieties of lettuce and leafy greens so really no reason to get bored. A serving is 1 cup and everyone should strive for one cup per day minimum. More if you are constipated as lettuce and leafy greens are a great source of fiber.

Chew very well as always. This helps your body absorb all the good stuff.

Cold or hot! There are many different ways to serve lettuce and leafy greens as you will come to discover throughout this book.

What nutrients do green leafy lettuces and greens have to offer? As it turns out, quite a bit. . .

These vegetables are a great source of:

- Fiber
- Water
- Carotenoids
- Vitamin C
- Folate
- Copper
- Biotin
- B1
- B2
- B6
- Iron
- Calcium
- Magnesium
- Potassium

And they contain zero or very low carbs.

Leaf lettuce (green) is the most nutritious. There is a red variety hence the distinction. Having said that, cold lettuce varieties run a very tight race on who is the most nutritious. So choose what you like. Mix and match your iceberg, romaine, leaf, bibb and watercress however you like.

Spinach, kale, and Swiss chard are the most nutritious of the dark green leafy vegetables that we tend to cook but again it's a pretty tight race. I would suggest not getting fixated on just one variety and eating it daily. I would mix it up from one week to the next.

If you have thyroid disease you will want to make sure you limit consumption of cruciferous vegetables to those that have been cooked only. They don't have to be mushy, but at least cooked till tender or just wilted. Leafy vegetables that are cruciferous need just a quick sauté'. They include: kale, cabbage, collards, and mustard greens. Cook them long enough that it does not feel raw to you when you eat them.

Lettuce Cups and The Lettuce Bun

I remember years ago hearing about a restaurant that was selling a hamburger using lettuce as the bun instead of a traditional bread bun. I thought that was crazy. Then I tried it. It's so good! Everyone I have convinced to at least try it, even men, have remarked how surprised they were that it was really good and continue to choose the lettuce bun at least on a regular basis if not every time.

I mean why would it be strange? If you have ever put lettuce on your hamburger then the food combination certainly is not foreign. Iceberg lettuce works best since they are already kind of round and the broadest in diameter. Layer two or three individual leaves for the top bun, and same for the bottom bun. Use scissors (keep some in the kitchen designated for food only) to cut the limpy end of the leaf off, or to shape the leaf. Save those leaf ends for making Green on Green Salad Dressing, Italian Sauce, pesto, and Lettuce Soup.

Choose a Lettuce Bun for your:

- Hamburger
- chicken sandwich
- fish sandwich
- pulled chicken sandwich
- Roasted Portobello Mushroom Sandwich.
- Anywhere you would normally use a bun

The Lettuce Cup

A fairly new thing that has been catching on and I just love it. What an easy and affordable way to cut calories, omit gluten and raise nutritional value in one's diet. Again, I think I was a little slow to catch on but now that I have I am putting everything in lettuce cups. I have always included lettuce on the top of my tacos so why not under them instead? Right?

Like the bun, when using iceberg lettuce layering is key and use your scissors to shape it just right.

Iceberg, Endive, or Romaine leaves work well as a lettuce cup for:
- Tacos
- Seasoned Chicken Tenders
- Marinated Steak
- Tuna Salad
- Egg Salad
- Italian Seasoned Ground Pork
- Chicken Salad
- Watermelon and Spinach Salad
- Grilled Chicken or Grilled Vegetables
- Fish tacos
- Asian Seasoned Steak
- Dips and Hummus

If you cook for more than just yourself there is nothing wrong with putting options on the table. You actually take options away when it is not made available. No one can make a healthy choice if it is not offered in the first place. Start small so that you don't waste food.

You choose the lettuce as your bun or in place of your taco shell and let others choose the traditional bread bun or processed corn and flour shells if they want. Don't act like it's any big thing on your part. Just remark that you saw this and wanted to try it as a way to cut back on bread. Then remark at how good it is. Nobody likes it when you try to talk them into eating something different. Keep putting it out. You keep eating it your way and someone may surprise you and want to try it one day.

Greens You Can Cook

- Spinach
- Kale
- Romaine
- Bok choy
- Cabbage
- Iceberg, etc. Yes you can cook these varieties of lettuce!

Certainly there are many leafy greens that are in your produce department and indeed many are in the freezer section of your grocery store. Take some extra time next week to browse. Look up some recipes and see what you might like to incorporate.

Over the past five years I have made an effort to try one new vegetable a month. And on occasion a new fruit. Sometimes I might try a vegetable or fruit I don't particularly care for but I have found a new recipe and want to try it prepared differently to see if I like it that way instead.

I have thoroughly enjoyed trying these new foods. It has been not only an adventure for the palette but I have pushed the boundaries of my cooking skills. Some were known to me but for some reason I simply had never had the opportunity to eat them.

I also made it a priority to try all the different lettuce varieties and dark green leafy's that my produce department has to offer. This takes about a full year as not all green leafy vegetables are available all year 'round. So keep checking week after week, month after month and each new season for the possibility of something new.

I scoured the web and cookbooks for how others were preparing their lettuce's and greens. Indian food, Mexican food, American food, Italian food, regional favorites and so on. Then I played with the idea and created new recipes that would be approved for those following the 5 Points Diet Plan. That means every recipe has to be gluten free, dairy free, nightshade free, soy free and grain free.

The point is to explore the vegetables in your produce department. Find out what all your store offers. If you aren't familiar with the produce department the foods change every month or so due to what is in season or not. Some produce departments have recipe cards near like foods. Everyone is familiar with green beans but have you ever bought fresh green beans from the produce department? I keep a can of green beans in the cupboard as well as frozen whole green beans in the freezer, but in the summer I buy fresh green beans. They each have their own "best preparation" recipes so it's really like 3 different vegetables to me.

Do the same in your freezer department. Take some extra time every few weeks and find out what all they offer. Find out what's new every now and then.

When buying frozen foods choose vegetables that do not have other ingredients added. No sauce, spices or seasonings.

What do I keep in my freezer?

- Green peas
- Chopped kale
- Chopped spinach
- Broccoli
- Cauliflower
- Peas and carrots

- Medley of celery, carrots and onion

These are some of the vegetables I keep in the freezer at all times and the rest gets rotated. Sometimes I get green beans, or whole okra, mushrooms, asparagus, and so on.

Check the freezer section of your local grocery store to see what kinds of greens they sell in the freezer section. Kale, spinach, collards, turnip greens, mustard greens.

You can make all kinds of things with frozen greens, straight from the freezer, it's fast and simple:

- Cream of Kale Soup
- Pesto's
- Add frozen chopped greens to soups, sauces and dressings
- Chimichurri sauce, dips and more.

Salad Recipes

If you find yourself bored with salads I encourage you to start by looking at the variety of lettuce listed on page five.

Take the time to browse the varieties of lettuce available in your grocery store. This will change with each season so it is a good idea to look each week to see what is available.

Check your favorite recipe sites for recipes that include different kinds of lettuce that you know are available at your regular grocery store.

Every week I buy two greens. One for cold use and one for hot. Whatever lettuce and/or greens you purchase be sure you have a plan to use them. Plan your meals for that week so that you will use the lettuce and greens in your meals within the next six to seven days. If something happens and you have lettuce or greens left that start to look like they are beginning to wilt or the leaves have started to turn a bit brown don't worry. That's when you make a dressing, dip, pesto, soup or sauce out of those leaves.

Your goal should be to eat a green leafy food every single day for optimal health.

I hope this book gives you enough variations and preparation ideas for lettuce and greens so that you can see how easy it can be to eat lettuce every day and not feel bored.

Green leafy foods, as mentioned above, are a great source of fiber. Fiber from green leafy vegetables do not generally cause some of the problems many people are having when they try to get their daily fiber from whole wheat glutens and grains. If you have a problem with constipation that isn't cured by eating whole grains I encourage you to try greens. All have fiber but the darker the green the more fiber it will deliver. To help your body absorb all the fiber be sure you are thoroughly chewing each bite.

We use to get told that lettuce is mostly "just" water. Guess what? It is. Then we found out our bodies need quite a bit of water each day. Its great news that we can eat our water as well as drink our water. Drinking water is more beneficial to your kidneys while eating foods that are high in water content is good for absorption in the remaining organs, including your skin. Water that is eaten through foods has time to be absorbed and used as the majority of it is absorbed as opposed to passing through like actual water. Both are good; just for different reasons.

Foods that contain high amounts of water that are dairy free, gluten free, grain free, nightshade free and soy free are:

- Cucumbers are 96% water
- Iceberg Lettuce is 95% water
- Butter head lettuce is 93% water
- Green Leaf lettuce is 89%
- Romaine is 87%
- Celery 95%
- Radishes are 95% water as well
- Cauliflower (if you don't squeeze it out) is 92% water
- Watermelon 91%
- Spinach is 91% water
- Star fruit 91%
- Strawberries 91%
- Raspberries, blueberries, and blackberries average 86.5% water
- Broccoli is 91%
- Carrots 89%
- And Cantaloupe is 90% water

So slice, puree, cube and bite into these foods and leave those other processed, unhealthy foods behind.

Salad Recipes and Ideas

Caesar Salad

Caesar Salad is a beautiful bed of Romaine Lettuce with a very distinct Caesar Dressing. Caesar dressing can easily be made at home so that you have control over the ingredients. A much healthier choice! This is a gluten free, dairy free, soy free and nightshade free version which taste exactly the same!

Caesar Salad Dressing:

- 2 Large Egg yolks
- 3 Anchovies (you can freeze the leftover anchovies in a glass jar)
- 1 or 2 Garlic cloves
- 2 Tablespoons (at least) Lemon Juice (I sometimes use lime juice too)
- ¾ teaspoon Dijon Mustard
- ½ cup plus 2 Tablespoons Oil
- Course Black Pepper
- Salt

Whisk egg yolks until silky smooth. Add a teaspoon or less at a time of the oil while continuing to whisk. Continue to slowly drizzle in all ½ cup of oil into the egg yolks. Egg yolks should be thick and glossy. Whisk in lemon juice and the Dijon mustard

In a small bowl mash anchovies with minced garlic and a pinch of salt. Whisk into the egg yolks.

Add black pepper and stir. Taste and adjust any seasonings and lemon juice as necessary.

Cover and refrigerate for at least an hour.

If you are concerned about the fish taste of the anchovies please don't be. I am not a fan of fishy smelling or tasting seafood myself but I like this dressing. The lemon juice changes the taste of the anchovies that comes through to cause the very distinct taste you find in a Caesar Dressing.

Oriental Salad

Ingredients:

- Basic Lettuce Puree
- Sesame Seed Oil
- Minced or ground Ginger
- Minced Garlic
- Minced fresh ginger or ground ginger
- Honey
- Oil
- Napa Cabbage
- Red Cabbage
- Carrots
- Scallions
- Mandarin Orange sections
- Salted Peanuts
- Cooked Chicken strips (breast)

Tear or shred Napa cabbage, red cabbage, grated carrots, scallions, and combine with Mandarin orange sections, salted peanuts and sliced cooked chicken.

Dressing: whisk together Basic Lettuce Puree, garlic, ginger, 1 1/2 teaspoons sesame oil, honey to taste. Pour dressing over salad and toss to combine.

American Salad

- Chopped lettuce; a crispy variety like Iceberg, Romaine, or Boston Head Lettuce
- Shredded Carrots
- Sliced Radishes

Toss with oil, salt and course black pepper. Drizzle with vinegar to taste.

Kale Salad with Peanut Dressing

- 1 to 2 lbs of kale
- 1 large carrot, peeled
- 3/4 cup roasted, salted peanuts, divided
- 1/3 cup oil
- 3 tablespoons apple cider vinegar
- 1 tablespoon brown sugar
- 1/2 teaspoon coarse salt

Remove the center rib of each piece of kale. Discard ribs. Stack the leaves. Roll them and then slice in half lengthwise, then crosswise into very fine strips. Put the leaves and 1/2 the peanuts in a large bowl.

Slice the carrot very thin, either by creating curls with a peeler, or by running the halved carrot lengthwise down a mandolin or use the side slicer on your grater. Add to the kale and peanuts.

In a food processor, briefly puree the remaining 1/4 cup peanuts, oil, vinegar, and sugar. Taste and add salt if needed. Pulse it just a few times; the peanuts should be partially pureed.

Toss dressing with the kale, nuts and carrots. Refrigerate for at least an hour.

Mixed Greens Salad

Prepackaged mixed greens is the easiest way to get a variety of leafy tender lettuce varieties without the expense of buying four different types yourself. The varieties vary, but usually contain some combination of baby romaine lettuce, Swiss chard, arugula, Frisee, and baby red leaf. These tender, not crisp, mixed varieties work great for topping your entrée rather than serving as an appetizer.

Always be sure to toss the mixed greens in your dressing before topping your entrée.

Steak Salad with Horseradish Dressing

Ingredients:

- Leftover steak sliced
- Basic Lettuce Puree (recipe on page 30)
- Horseradish
- Lemon juice
- Bibb lettuce, chopped or torn
- Thinly sliced radishes
- Purple or red grapes, halved (I tried green and they don't really work in this recipe)
- Fresh chives, chopped

Combine the BLP (basic lettuce puree) with horseradish and lime juice to taste. Thin out with oil if needed for a dressing consistency. Should be think enough to drizzle and toss like any other salad dressing you would use.

Chop and slice lettuce, radishes, and grapes and toss in a bowl.

Toss with the Horseradish dressing. Top it all off with the steak. Sprinkle with the chopped chives and a dollop of the horseradish dressing.

Bonus: as a bonus I like to add fried onions to this dish. Dip sliced onion in egg whites. Not the whole egg but just the egg white. Fry until a golden brown.

Taco Salad

Always make plenty of chopped lettuce available when making taco salad. The extra thing to do here is to also make lettuce cups available to use instead of a taco shell or for use instead of nacho chips. Let's face it, taco meat and toppings are quite good simply put on a bed of lettuce too! No shells or nachos needed.

Pickled Onion and Cucumber Spinach Salad

- Thinly sliced cucumber. Use the side slicer on your grater.
- Thinly sliced red onion
- Apple cider vinegar
- A sprinkling of white sugar or stevia
- Salt and coarse black pepper
- Fresh Spinach leaves

Place the onion and cucumber in a jar with the vinegar, salt and pepper. Close, shake and set in refrigerator for at least an hour.

When you are ready to serve, toss the pickled cucumber and onions with fresh spinach leaves and about some of the vinegar (to taste) along with drizzled oil. Toss well so that all leaves are coated.

Chopped Salad

This salad has a lot of repetitive vegetables from other salads but if you have never tried it I encourage you to just once and see what you think. There is something about cutting the vegetables differently that changes the dynamic of this salad.

Start with a crispy lettuce variety like iceberg or romaine. Choose vegetables that are crisp or firm like carrots, radishes, beets, cucumbers, onion, and jicama.

Chop everything to about the same size and preferably about the size of an olive or smaller.

Toss well with your favorite dressing.

Seared Romaine Salad

- Romaine Hearts cut in half lengthwise
- Rough Chopped Yellow Onion
- 1 can Artichoke Hearts rough chopped
- 2 garlic cloves
- Small amount of crispy fried bacon crumbles (equivalent of just one half strip per each Romaine half). This is optional. I make this many times and omit the bacon.
- Black iron skillet, grill or you can put this under the broiler

Drizzle oil in skillet. Sauté the onion in a hot black iron skillet until softened. Add one artichoke heart for each romaine heart. Sauté the onion, garlic and artichoke hearts in the skillet until tender. Drizzle with apple cider vinegar and stir around until strong smell of vinegar disappears. About one minute. Remove from skillet. Now use the skillet to sear your romaine hearts.

Drizzle oil on romaine hearts and sprinkle with salt and pepper. Sear in hot lightly oiled black iron skillet until browned. Anywhere from 2-5 minutes.

Top the romaine heart with the onion, artichoke and garlic mix.

I have also seared iceberg lettuce and thought it also tasted great.

Mediterranean Chopped Salad

- Chopped leaf lettuce
- Chopped artichoke hearts
- Chopped black olives
- Chopped green olives (without pimento)
- Chopped peeled cucumber
- Chopped fresh basil leaves
- Thinly sliced radishes
- Chopped fresh parsley
- Minced garlic cloves
- Oil
- Vinegar of your choice
- Oregano
- Salt and pepper

Mix oil, vinegar, oregano, garlic cloves, salt and pepper in a glass jar and refrigerate while you prepare the vegetables.

The ratio of vegetables you want to use is a preference. Toss the entire salad with the dressing for best results. This is very good with seared steak on top!

Wedge Salad

Cut a head of iceberg lettuce into 4 wedges.

Dressing Ingredients:

- Basic Lettuce Puree
- Vinegar
- Italian Seasoning or Course Black Pepper
- Small amount of crisp crumbled bacon

Combine all ingredients, adjust to taste and pour over each wedge.

Layered Salad

This is my version of the Seven Layer American Salad. This is nightshade and dairy free gluten free, soy free and grain free.

1. Chopped iceberg lettuce
2. Frozen Green Peas
3. Avocado
4. Chopped Cucumber
5. Chopped Cilantro or Parsley
6. Chopped Boiled Eggs
7. Chopped Bacon (mark on your wall calendar any time you eat cured meats in an effort to limit consumption)

Salads have an unlimited degree of variety. There is also no one way to prepare a salad. Salads while typically served chilled don't necessarily have to be served cold. There are many room temperature salads and even some that are served sautéed, grilled or broiled.

Lettuce Recipes

Basic Lettuce Puree

Ingredients:

- 1 cup chopped Iceberg lettuce
- 3-4 tablespoons oil
- 3-4 tablespoons water
- Salt and pepper

Blend together. Great to eat right away as a sandwich spread or salad dressing but gets even better when put in the refrigerator for a bit. You can, of course, add Italian seasonings and your favorite vinegar for an Italian Dressing.

Add Cilantro and Lime for a Southwest flavor profile for taco salad dressing.

Sesame Seed Oil, honey and Ginger for an Asian Spinach salad dressing or to toss with rice noodles for an Asian Noodle dish.

Add Italian seasoning for a great pesto, pizza sauce or use as a pasta sauce.

This is a very versatile basic starter puree that you can make from iceberg lettuce that is getting wilt-ee or starting to turn brown. Use all green and white parts. All but the very hard core.

As you look through the recipes in this book you will see many include the Basic Lettuce Puree.

In theory you can use any lettuce you have on hand. Depending on which lettuce variety you choose will depend on the flavor you end up with. I prefer Iceberg as it is one of the sweeter tasting lettuce varieties. But you could of course use Romaine for a more bitter taste.

Pork Sandwich Horseradish Spread

- Basic Iceberg Puree (page 30)
- Turmeric to taste
- Horseradish to taste

Blend until very smooth and use as a spread for shredded pork or steak lettuce cups or tortilla wrap. Also good on Gluten Free Steak Flatbread.

Green on Green Salad Dressing:

- One cup chopped Iceberg lettuce.
- Two teaspoons water
- Small squirt of Apple Cider Vinegar
- ½ teaspoon Dijon mustard
- Dash of salt and pepper
- 1/8 cup oil

Blend all till smooth and creamy. You have to pulse it on and off to get it started. Once it does start to blend it will liquefy very quickly. Add more vinegar, seasonings to taste. If too thick add oil or water.

If too thin add more chopped lettuce or add a chopped cucumber (no need to peel) or you could even add an avocado.

Best when chilled for at least an hour. Will store fine in a glass jar in the refrigerator for a week.

Lettuce Soup

- 2 T. Oil
- 1 T diced onion
- 2 chopped garlic cloves
- 1 T chopped parsley or cilantro
- 1 Iceberg head of lettuce or Romaine
- 3 cups good chicken stock
- Salt and pepper to taste

Combine chicken stock, garlic cloves, salt, and lettuce to blender or food processor. Blend till a rustic consistency or until smooth; whatever your preference. Allow to sit while you sauté the onion. In a saucepan add 2 tablespoons oil, add 2 tablespoons diced onion.
Sauté' onion till onion is translucent. Transfer soup from blender to saucepan and heat through. Allow to simmer on low for about 15 minutes.

Variations:
You could add cooked diced cauliflower (or frozen chopped up to diced size) when you add the chives.
This also makes a great sauce for chicken or pork chops.

Cucumber Spinach Dip

- 2 cups fresh spinach
- ¼ cup chopped cucumber (you can leave the peel on)
- Oil to consistency: start with 4 tablespoons
- 2 tablespoons water
- Salt, pepper to taste
- 2 garlic cloves
- 1 teaspoon Dijon mustard (optional)
- Apple Cider Vinegar to taste (optional)
- Dill or Italian seasonings depending on your preference (optional)

Place spinach, cucumber, oil, water, garlic salt and pepper in blender. Blend. Taste to see what other seasonings and/or vinegar you may want to add. Best when chilled for at least an hour prior to serving. This is wonderful as a spread for a sandwich, tortilla wrap, hamburger or a smear on a plate under a nice white fish.

Pesto

A standard pesto recipe has pine nuts so add those if you like them. I have never put them in my pesto and have never missed them. Parmesan cheese is also optional. Yes, it does make a difference in the taste but if you are eating dairy free omitting it still leaves you with a great tasting pesto; just a slightly different taste. I find substituting a little Dijon mustard gives the pesto that tangy salty flavor I am looking for from the missing parmesan.

- 2 cups fresh spinach leaves
- ¼ cup fresh basil leaves (optional) you can also use fresh cilantro in place of the basil
- 4 garlic cloves
- ¼ cup oil that you will add a little at a time to suit the consistency you like
- Salt and pepper
- Lime juice or lemon juice. If citrus bothers you use the zest instead of the juice or choose some apple cider vinegar.

Blend all ingredients and chill at least an hour to allow the flavors to marry.

Pesto is a great substitute for pasta sauce, pizza sauce if you are avoiding nightshades. Adding a can of drained chopped artichoke hearts after blending also makes it seem even more 'tomato-ee'.

Cilantro Lime Dressing

- .5 bunch fresh cilantro
- 2 limes juiced or 1/4c lime juice (start with small amount and add to taste)
- 1 clove garlic
- 2 T. Red Wine Vinegar
- ½ t. Dijon Mustard (yellow mustard and horseradish)
- ¼ c Oil
- Salt and Pepper

Blend in processor or blender until consistency you like. Some like a more rustic chunky chopped consistency while others prefer a smooth, fine consistency. For me it depends on what I will be using it for. Very good after given a chance to chill in refrigerator for at least an hour. Works very well to make ahead night or two before.

You could prepare the BLP (basic lettuce puree) and add this to it to make it go further. The Basic Lettuce Puree will take up the stronger flavor of the Cilantro and vinegar.

Cream of Kale Soup

- 2 cups frozen chopped kale (thawed)
- Chicken broth (be sure you are using a good strong stock)
- 2 tablespoons chopped onion
- Ground pork (about 6 tablespoons) browned and seasoned with oregano, salt and pepper (optional)
- ¼ teaspoon Dijon Mustard (optional)

If including the ground pork, start browning that while blending the vegetables and broth. While pork is browning:

Place thawed kale and onion into blender. Add about one cup of broth.

Blend till smooth or consistency you like. Add more broth if you want it thinner and more kale if you want it thicker.

Transfer contents in blender to the skillet with the browned seasoned pork. Or a saucepan on its own if not including the pork. Heat through.

Add lime zest or a squirt of apple cider vinegar. If you aren't sure that will taste good to you put a small amount of soup in a bowl, add a bit of vinegar or zest and see how you like it. Another option I like is adding a teaspoon of Dijon mustard instead of the lime or vinegar.

Green Garlicky Salad Dressing

- 2 cups Iceberg lettuce
- 3 garlic cloves
- Oil
- Salt and pepper
- Apple cider vinegar or Lime Juice

Put chopped lettuce, and garlic in blender with 1 tablespoon water

Use pulse to get the lettuce started adding a little bit of oil at a time until consistency you want. Add Vinegar to taste. This is also good with a small chopped scallion.

Best after chilling in refrigerator for at least an hour.

Lettuce Relish

Ingredients:

- Finely chopped lettuce
- Healthy Olive oil based mayo
- Mustard
- Salt and pepper

Mix well. This is especially complimentary to a chicken sandwich or turkey burger!

Basic Chicken Wing Dipping Sauce:

Ingredients:

- 1 cup Iceberg lettuce
- 1 garlic clove
- ½ teaspoon onion powder
- 4 Tablespoons oil
- Fruit: raspberries (frozen or fresh)
- Honey to taste

Blend well until pureed together. I found no reason to add salt or pepper but if you want some heat to eat pepper would not hurt the integrity of the recipe. This will keep in the refrigerator for several days in a glass jar. I like to save pesto jars, olive jars, and artichoke or small pickle jars for homemade things like this.

Now you could substitute your fruit of choice here. I think raspberries work best and they are very easy to find frozen. If you make raspberry jam you could also use that. If you do use a jam or jelly you have put up (canned yourself) please omit the honey as it will already be sweetened.

The lettuce lowers the "per serving" sugar content, lowers the calories per serving and raises the fiber and Vitamins you get per serving.

Sweet and Sour Sauce

Ingredients:

- Pineapple chunks – 1 can
- Chopped White Onion
- ¼ cup thinly sliced celery

Basic Chicken Wing Dipping Sauce Recipe: you can use raspberries for a red sweet and sour sauce or substitute a can of drained, rinsed apricots for a yellow/orange sweet and sour sauce.

- Vinegar to taste
- Adjust onion powder to taste
- One teaspoon white sugar
- Honey to taste only if not sweet enough

The lettuce in the Basic Chicken Wing Dipping Sauce gives this body, and lends a mild bell pepper taste. If you use Romaine or other lettuce variety it will change the taste of the recipe. I think the iceberg works best here as it is a slightly sweet lettuce variety. However, use what you prefer. Some like a peppery taste like what you would achieve if you used Arugula or Mustard Greens. You could always use a blend of Iceberg and one of the peppery lettuce varieties.

Directions:

Make the Basic Chicken Wing Dipping Sauce once you have chosen the fruit flavor profile you want (raspberry or apricot). Add 1 tablespoon apple cider vinegar, one teaspoon white sugar, another shake of onion powder and blend until smooth. Add equal parts water and oil if needed to create a smooth saucy texture.

In a skillet sauté onion, celery and pineapple chunks or tidbits in small amount of oil or a few tablespoons of chicken or vegetable broth. Sauté` until just tender. Add sauce and cover. Allow to simmer about 15 minutes.

Use as a sweet and sour sauce over chicken or pork.

Spinach and Onion Sauté

- 4 cups fresh spinach
- ½ cup sliced onion
- Oil, salt and pepper
- Apple Cider Vinegar

This is especially good made in a skillet using the renderings after cooking a steak, chop or chicken breast.

Add oil to skillet and sauté the onions until tender. Add spinach and stir until wilted. Salt and pepper. Remove from heat. Drizzle with vinegar.

Spinach and Mushroom Sauté'

- Cooking oil
- 2 cloves garlic finely diced
- 2 Tablespoons Chicken Broth
- ½ teaspoon Dijon Mustard
- 2 Cups Fresh Spinach
- 1 Cup fresh mushrooms
- Salt and Pepper

Toss mushrooms in oil, salt and pepper. Sauté' mushrooms in skillet until rendered. Put the mushrooms in a cold skillet and cook until golden brown for a deeper flavor. Add chopped garlic halfway through mushrooms cooking. Add at least 1-2 cups fresh spinach leaves and stir until spinach is just wilted; about a minute or two. Remove from heat.

If you feel you need some liquid while cooking add a couple tablespoons of chicken broth. You can easily elevate this dish by using several different types of mushrooms in this one dish as well as two or more types of hearty greens, like spinach and kale or spinach and mustard greens. The mustard greens have a sort of pepper taste that would change the dynamic of this dish slightly.

Tartar Sauce (eggless, dairy free, gluten free, soy free and nightshade free)

- BLP (basic lettuce puree)
- Chopped/diced dill pickle
- Small amount of finely diced white onion
- Minced anchovy (optional)
- lemon juice

Mix all together. Taste. Add salt if needed. Best when refrigerated for several hours.

Spinach Frittata

- 4 Eggs whisked together in a bowl with 2 tablespoons water
- 1 tablespoon real butter or ghee
- 1 teaspoon diced onion (optional)
- 1 cup fresh spinach
- thyme
- Salt and Pepper

Melt a tablespoon of real butter or ghee with a drizzle of oil in the skillet.
Add about a teaspoon of diced onion. Sauté' till tender. Add fresh spinach and stir till coated. Add thyme and stir. Break eggs into separate bowl and beat, add 2 tablespoons water. Pour over top vegetables in skillet. Cover on med heat. Check every 3 minutes.

Healing Leafy Chicken Soup

Ingredients:

- 2 chicken thighs, bone in and skin on.
- Dark green leafy like spinach or kale; chopped or torn
- Bay leaf
- Thyme (don't cut corners when it comes to thyme. Buy a good quality brand)
- Garlic clove (You can freeze garlic cloves. Just set them in a freezer bag. Use as needed)

Brown 2 chicken thighs on both sides. Place in slow cooker and cover with water. Add bay leaf, garlic clove and sprinkle in some Thyme. Cook on high about 2 hours until chicken appears done. Add about ½ cup frozen diced onions, celery, carrots mix and continue to cook on high 30 minutes. Remove the chicken and allow to cool enough to handle. Remove bone and skin. Using fork, shred chicken or use a knife and cut into bite size pieces depending on your preference. Return to the crock pot.

Just before serving remove the bay leaf and add chopped or torn dark green. If you are adding a soft green like spinach it will wilt immediately. If you are adding a hearty ddark green such as kale you will need it to cook about 5 to 10 minutes before serving.

Grilled Romaine

If the Romaine Hearts are large, cut in half lengthwise. Drizzle all sides with oil, salt and pepper. Put under the broiler until starts to brown.

Braised Lettuce and Peas

Ingredients:

- Chicken Broth
- Real butter or ghee
- Gluten free flour or Arrowroot (about 2 tablespoons)
- Couple tablespoons diced onion
- 1 cup frozen green peas
- 1 cup chopped lettuce (iceberg, romaine, bibb, leaf)
- Optional: apple cider vinegar
- Optional: Thyme seasoning is especially good in this dish.

Drizzle oil in pan. Add butter to melt. Add the gf flour or Arrowroot and stir around, then slowly pour in chicken stock. Continue to stir as it will thicken. Keeping it at a simmer add onions, frozen peas and chopped lettuce. Add salt and pepper to taste. Simmer for about 5 minutes. Some like a squirt of apple cider vinegar for brightness after removing from heat.

Pea, Lettuce and Fennel Soup

Ingredients:

- Shallots or a mild onion (2 small) - chopped
- 1 medium fennel bulb – chopped, about 2 cups
- 1 medium head of Bibb lettuce; chopped
- 10 ounce pkg frozen green peas
- 1.5 cups chicken broth

Sauté onion and fennel in butter. Add salt and pepper, cover, and simmer on medium heat about 5 minutes.

Add broth (keeping about ½ cup reserved) and stir until completely combined. Remove from heat. Add lettuce and frozen peas, toss until lettuce is wilted.

Transfer to another bowl and allow to cool about 20 minutes.

Transfer to blender and do a rustic blend unless you are looking for a silky smooth consistency; then blend until completely smooth.

Transfer back into the saucepan to heat through.

Taste and adjust seasonings.

Chimichurri

- Fresh parsley or cilantro
- Oregano
- Garlic
- Oil
- Red wine vinegar (or apple cider vinegar)

Combine all. Allow to sit at least 30 minutes. Best served at room temperature. Can be stored 5 days in the refrigerator. Best in glass jar. When you want to serve it, allow the chimichurri to become room temperature again. Generally used on meat.

Honey Mustard Lettuce Bed

Chop Romaine lettuce to bite size pieces. Toss with Honey Mustard to coat all the leaves. Put a nice layer on the plate and top with a Baked, grilled or sautéed chicken breast.

Honey Mustard:
Mix equal parts honey with prepared yellow mustard. Adjust amounts to taste. Make extra to drizzle on top of the hot sizzling chicken breast.

Buttery Garlic Seafood Sauce

- ½ cup Basic Lettuce Puree (page 30)
- ¼ cup melted Real Butter or Ghee
- One or more garlic cloves, minced
- Salt

Combine all ingredients except salt and heat through. Taste before adding salt. Especially if you use salted butter. Cover and let sit 15 minutes. Use on any seafood. Traditionally one would just add garlic to melted butter for lobster or any seafood such as baked salmon or cod or perhaps to make a shrimp scampi. By adding the Basic Lettuce Puree you are adding nutrients and you are lowering the per serving fat and sodium.

Other Leafy Greens You Should Eat More of. . .

All leafy green vegetables are free foods; like celery.

The leaves on the celery, a leafy green, are wonderful for eating and look beautiful in soups and sauces! Parsley, cilantro, basil and mint plants are great green leafy's to grow in your kitchen or on the patio in a container.

- Cilantro: Not just for salsa and guacamole. Chop a big handful and add to your salad, to your frittata, to a sauce or to a homemade dressing.
- Parsley: Grab a hand full, not a pinch.

  Use for a garnish, and use in salads, sauces, chimichurri, and pesto!
  Fresh parsley is wonderful in a salad, chopped for a sauce, a frittata or omelet. Also great for making homemade salad dressings. Toss with fresh vegetables like a cucumber salad.
- All greens – spinach, kale, mustard greens, turnip greens, collard greens.
- Celery leaves
- Carrot top greens
- Basil leaves: make pesto, tear basil leaves and put on top of a pizza

•

In Conclusion

Would you mind taking a moment to review this book on Amazon? Your review helps this book become more visible on Amazon.

Follow my Amazon's Author page and get a notification when I release my next book. Your support, reading, lending, sharing and review of this book means so much to me. Thank you.

I am always available for discussion and questions on my Amazon author's page. www.Amazon.com/author/paulachenderson

From the Authors Page; just scroll down a bit on the page. You will find 'Customer Discussions' area.

Or catch up with me on social networking. Just look for the hashtag #5ptsfreediet

Other Books By Paula C. Henderson available on Amazon in 13 Countries. . .

- What's Left To Eat? The 5 Points Diet Grocery List
  ASIN: pending

- Tips For Weight Loss Success ~ You Can Do This!
  ASIN: B01LYVVC1S

- All You Can Eat Free Foods: A Specialty List Companion of the 5 Points Diet Plan
  ASIN: B01M0GHPXG

- Dictionary of Cooking Terms: For the Beginner Cook

  ASIN: B01L88R4EM

- How I Got Free Stuff To Sell On Ebay: And You Can Too!

  ASIN: B01KGP8FZU

Available in 13 countries.

1920x1043

Printed in Great Britain
by Amazon